PreTime® Piano

PRIMER LEVEL

Arranged by Nancy and Randall Faber

This book belongs to: _____

Production Coordinator: Jon Ophoff
Editor: Isabel Otero Bowen
Design: Terpstra Design, San Francisco
Engraving: Dovetree Productions, Inc.

Disney Characters and Artwork © Disney

FABER
PIANO ADVENTURES®

HAL•LEONARD®

A NOTE TO TEACHERS

PreTime® Piano Disney offers an exciting set of contemporary and classic Disney favorites, arranged for the Primer student. The selections provide excellent practice of basic rhythms and beginning note reading. The pieces span primarily Bass C to Treble G.

Teacher duets provide vitality and color. They can be played and enjoyed with the teacher, a parent, sibling, or advancing student.

PreTime® Piano Disney designates the Primer Level of the PreTime to BigTime Piano Supplementary Library arranged by Faber & Faber. The series allows students to enjoy a favorite style at their current level of study. PreTime books are available in these styles: *Popular, Classics, Jazz & Blues, Rock'n Roll, Ragtime & Marches, Hymns, Kids' Songs, Christmas,* and the *Faber Studio Collection*.

Visit us at **PianoAdventures.com**.

Helpful Hints:

1. The student should know his/her part well before attempting ensemble playing. However, the duet part can be used first to demonstrate the rhythmic feel or "groove" of the song.
2. When performed up-to-tempo, some of the pieces have a feeling of cut time. An effective approach to these pieces is to have the student begin with the quarter note at a moderate tempo and then work up to a fast quarter-note beat. This essentially provides "built-in" slow practice, while also meeting the student's need for a sense of speed and mastery.
3. The selections appear in approximate order of difficulty.
4. The student may go through several *PreTime* books, at the teacher's discretion, before moving up to *PlayTime Piano* (Level 1).

THE PRETIME TO BIGTIME PIANO LIBRARY

PreTime® Piano	=	Primer Level
PlayTime® Piano	=	Level 1
ShowTime® Piano	=	Level 2A
ChordTime® Piano	=	Level 2B
FunTime® Piano	=	Level 3A–3B
BigTime® Piano	=	Level 4 & above

ISBN 978-1-61677-697

Printed in U.S.A.

WARNING: The music, text, design, and graphics in this publication are protected by copyright law.
Any duplication is an infringement of U.S. copyright law.

FF3039

TABLE OF CONTENTS

I Just Can't Wait to Be King (from *The Lion King*) 4

It's a Small World (from Disney Parks' "it's a small world" Attraction) 6

Supercalifragilisticexpialidocious (from *Mary Poppins*) 8

Winnie the Pooh* (from *The Many Adventures of Winnie the Pooh*) 10

The Siamese Cat Song (from *Lady and the Tramp*) 12

I See the Light (from *Tangled*) 14

Do You Want to Build a Snowman? (from *Frozen*) 16

Scales and Arpeggios (from *The Aristocats*) 18

Step in Time (from *Mary Poppins*) 20

Music Dictionary 21

*Based on the "Winnie the Pooh" works, by A. A. Milne and E. H. Shepard

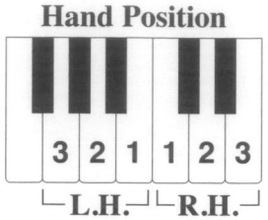

I Just Can't Wait to Be King

from *The Lion King*

Music by ELTON JOHN
Lyrics by TIM RICE

Happily

mf I'm gon - na be a might - y king, so en - e - mies be - ware! I've

5

nev - er seen a king of beasts with quite so lit - tle hair. Oh, I

Teacher Duet: (Student plays 1 octave higher)

R.H.

L.H.

mp

1. 2.

© 1994 Wonderland Music Company, Inc.
All Rights Reserved. Used by Permission.

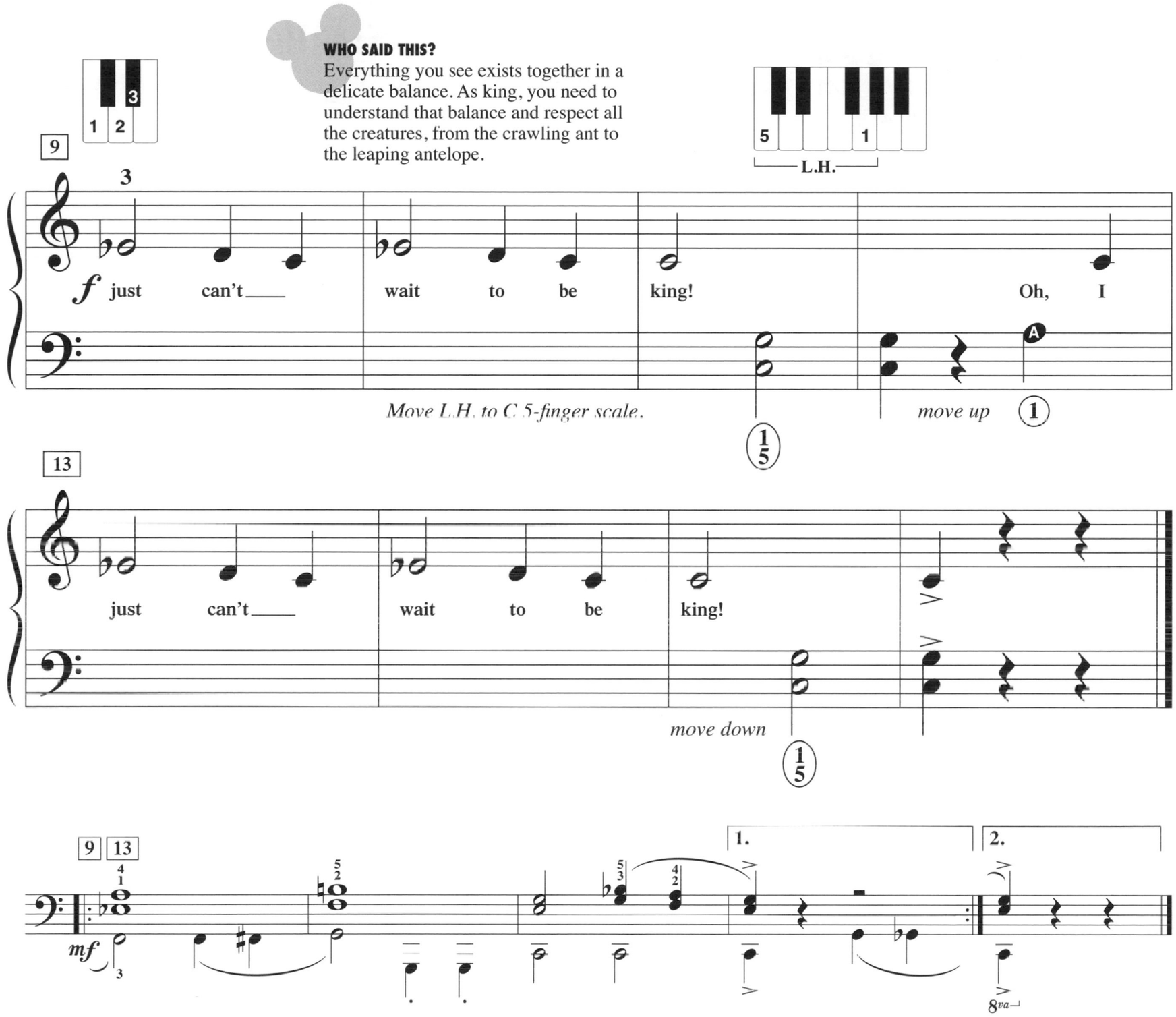
WHO SAID THIS?
Everything you see exists together in a delicate balance. As king, you need to understand that balance and respect all the creatures, from the crawling ant to the leaping antelope.
1 2 3
5 1
L.H.
9
3
f just can't wait to be king! Oh, I
A
Move L.H. to C 5-finger scale.
move up
1
1 5
13
just can't wait to be king!
move down
1 5
9 13
4 1
5 2
5 3
4 2
mf
3
1.
2.
8va
ANSWER: Mufasa

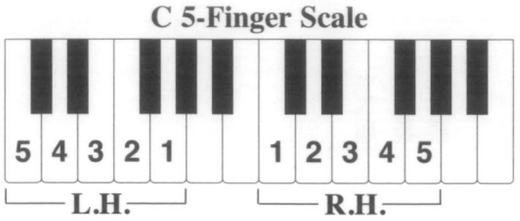

It's a Small World

from Disney Parks' "it's a small world" Attraction

Words and Music by
RICHARD M. SHERMAN
and ROBERT B. SHERMAN

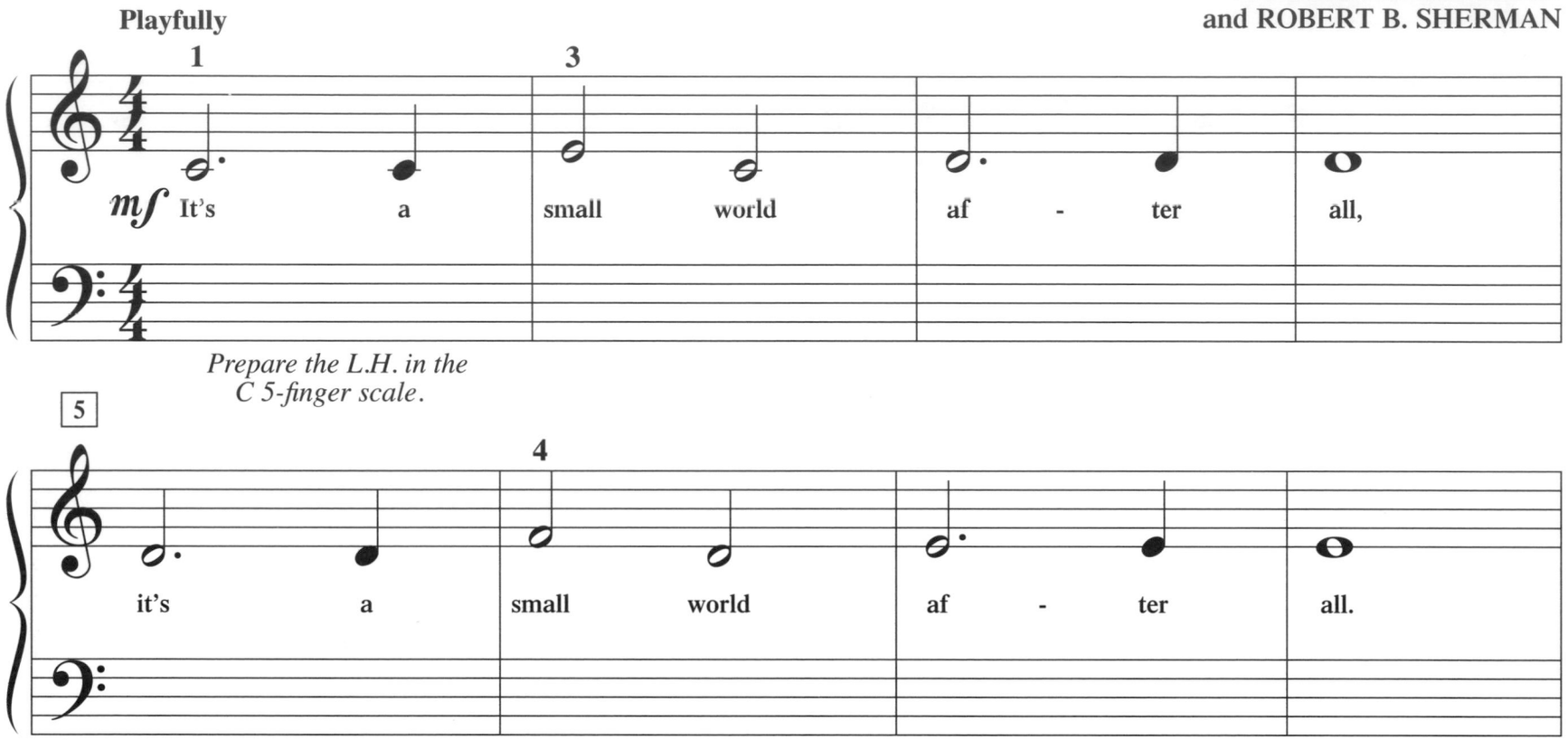

Teacher Duet: (Student plays 1 octave higher)

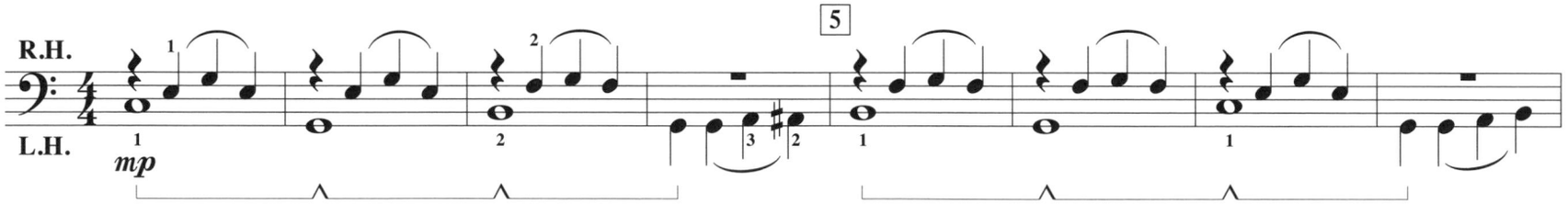

© 1963 Wonderland Music Company, Inc.
Copyright Renewed.
All Rights Reserved. Used by Permission.

DID YOU KNOW?
The music for this Disney ride first used many national anthems all playing together—rather confusing! In the Sherman brothers' autobiography *Walt's Time,* the songwriters recalled, "Walt told us, 'I need something, and I need something right away. It should talk about unity and understanding and brotherly love, but don't get preachy. And I need it yesterday because it has to be translated into a whole lot of different languages.' We wrote the song so fast, we thought it was too simple to play for Walt…It seems to have turned out pretty well."

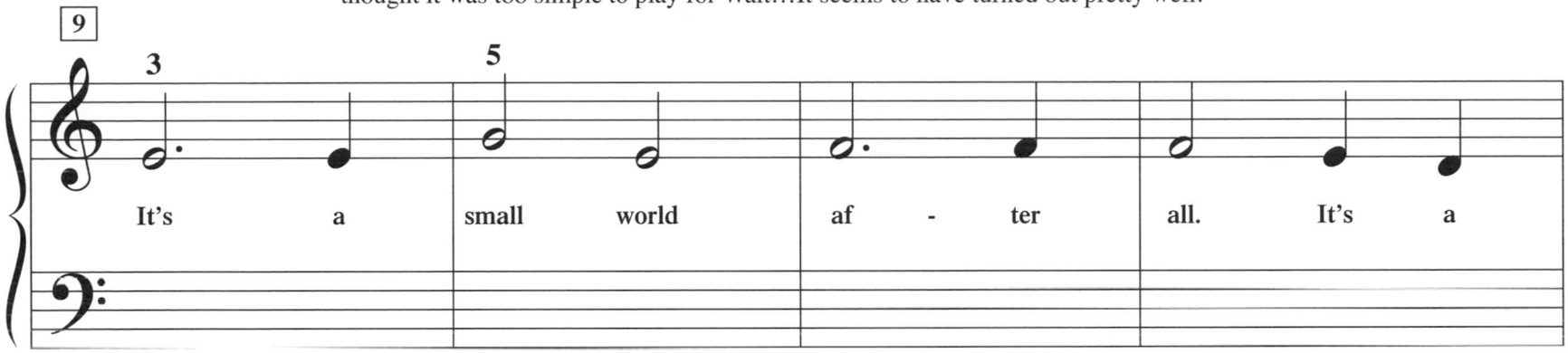

* For the duet the final low C for the student is optional.

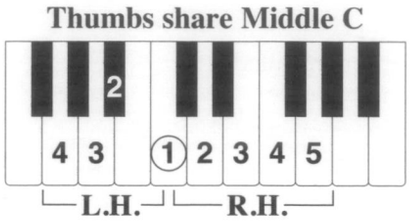

Supercalifragilisticexpialidocious

from *Mary Poppins*

Words and Music by
RICHARD M. SHERMAN
and ROBERT B. SHERMAN

Cheerfully

mf Sup - er - cal - i - frag - il - is - tic - ex - pi - al - i - do - cious!

5

E - ven though the sound of it is some - thing quite a - tro - cious,

Teacher Duet: (Student plays 1 octave higher)

R.H.

L.H.

mp

© 1963 Wonderland Music Company, Inc.
Copyright Renewed.
All Rights Reserved. Used by Permission.

WHO SAID THIS?
You know, you can say it backwards,
which is Dociousaliexpiisticfragicalirupes —
but that's going a bit too far, don't you think?

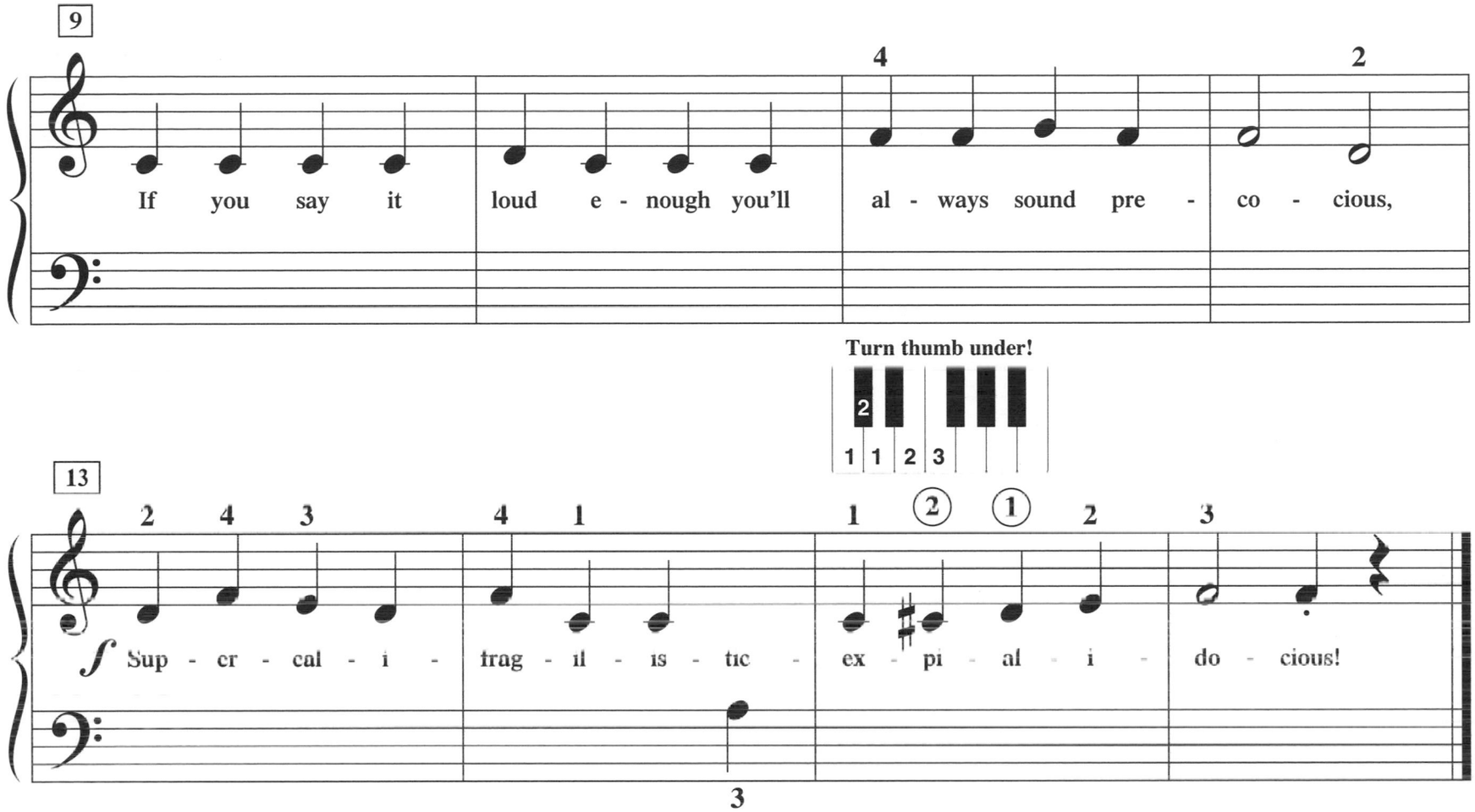

ANSWER: Mary Poppins

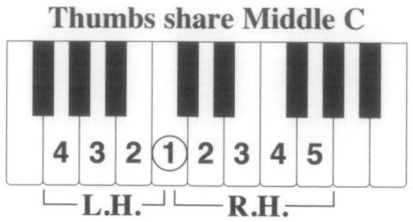

Winnie the Pooh*

from *The Many Adventures of Winnie the Pooh*

Words and Music by
RICHARD M. SHERMAN
and ROBERT B. SHERMAN

Happily

mf Win - nie the Pooh, Win - nie the Pooh.

5

Tub - by lit - tle cub - by all stuffed with fluff. He's

Teacher Duet: (Student plays 1 octave higher)

R.H.

L.H. *mp*

© 1963 Wonderland Music Company, Inc.
Copyright Renewed.
All Rights Reserved. Used by Permission.

*Based on the "Winnie the Pooh" works, by A. A. Milne and E. H. Shepard

ANSWER: Winnie the Pooh

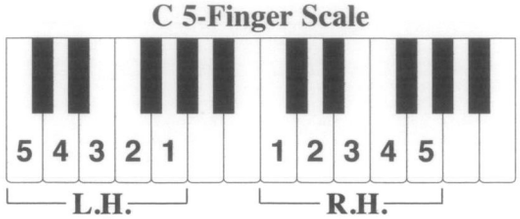

The Siamese Cat Song

from *Lady and the Tramp*

Words and Music by
PEGGY LEE and
SONNY BURKE

Rather slowly

mf We are Si - am - ee - iz if you plee - iz,

5

We are Si - am - ee - iz if you don't please.

Teacher Duet: (Student plays 2 octaves higher)

1 5

R.H.

L.H.

mp

1.

2.

© 1953 Walt Disney Music Company
Copyright Renewed.
All Rights Reserved. Used by Permission.

WHO SAID THIS?
Okay, okay, okay! But remember this, Pigeon. A human heart has only so much room for love and affection. When a baby moves in, the dog moves out.

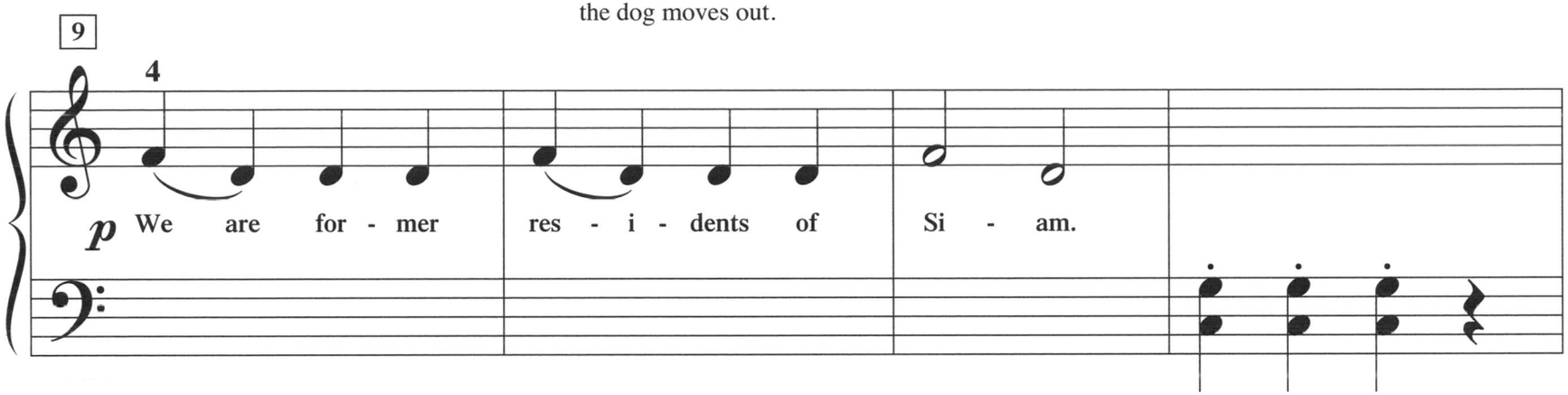

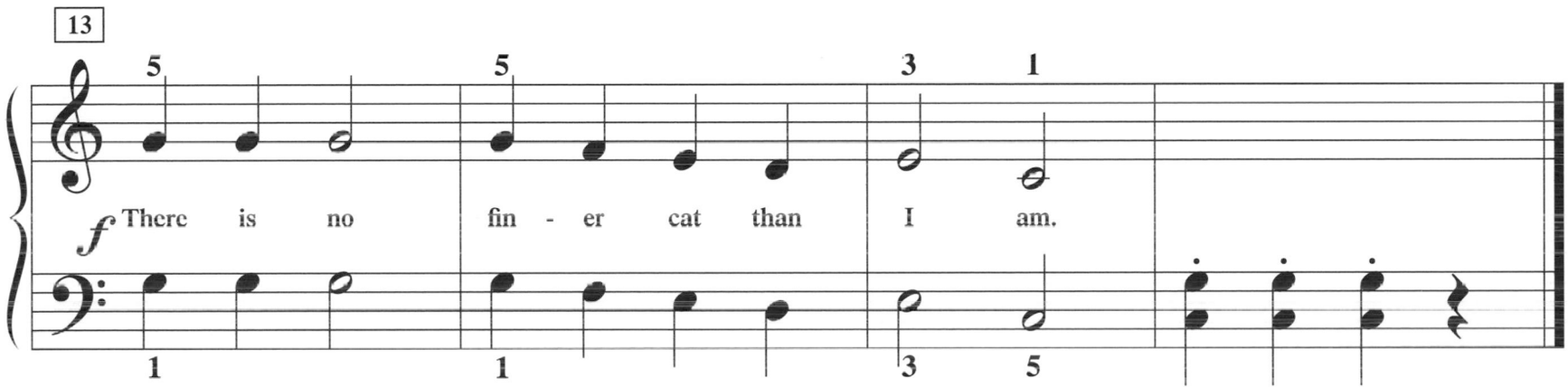

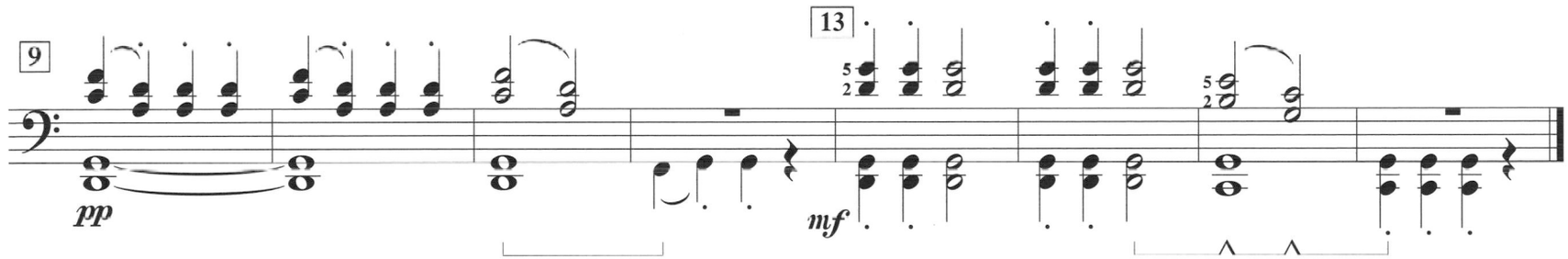

ANSWER: Tramp

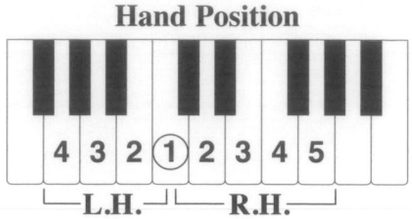

I See the Light

From Walt Disney's *TANGLED*

Music by ALAN MENKEN
Lyrics by GLENN SLATER

Flowing along

mf All those days, *(2 - 3 - 4)* watch - ing from the win - dows.

All those years, *(2 - 3 - 4)* out - side look - ing in. *(2 - 3 - 4)*

Move R.H. 3 up to A.

Teacher Duet: (Student plays 1 octave higher)

R.H.

L.H.

mp with pedal

mf

© 2010 Wonderland Music Company, Inc. and Walt Disney Music Company
All Rights Reserved. Used by Permission.

ANSWER: Rapunzel

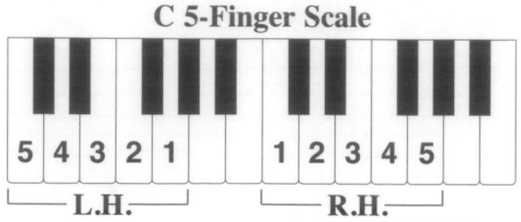

WHO SAID THIS?
Some people are worth melting for.

Do You Want to Build a Snowman?

from *Frozen*

Music and Lyrics by
KRISTEN ANDERSON-LOPEZ
and ROBERT LOPEZ

Moderately

mf Do you want to build a snow - man? Come on, let's go and play! *(2 - 3 - 4)*

Teacher Duet: (Student plays 1 octave higher)

R.H.

L.H.

mp

© 2013 Wonderland Music Company, Inc.
All Rights Reserved. Used by Permission.

9
(1 - 2) I nev - er see you an - y - more. (rest!) Come out the
13
door! (2 - 3) It's like you've gone a - way. (2 - 3 - 4 1 - 2 - 3 - 4)
grow louder
f
17
mf Do you want to build a snow - man?
p
13
17
pp

ANSWER: Olaf

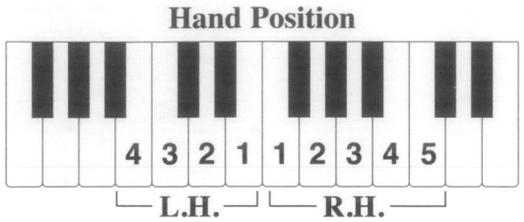

Scales and Arpeggios

from *The Aristocats*

Words and Music by
RICHARD M. SHERMAN
and ROBERT B. SHERMAN

Cheerfully

mp Ev - 'ry tru - ly cul - tured mu - sic stu - dent knows

Middle C 3 2 1

5

You must learn your scales and your ar - peg - gi - os.

4 1 1 3

Teacher Duet: (Student plays 1 octave higher)

R.H. only

p

© 1968 Wonderland Music Company, Inc.
Copyright Renewed.
All Rights Reserved. Used by Permission.

WHO SAID THIS?
Thank you, Miss Frou-Frou,
for letting me ride on your back.

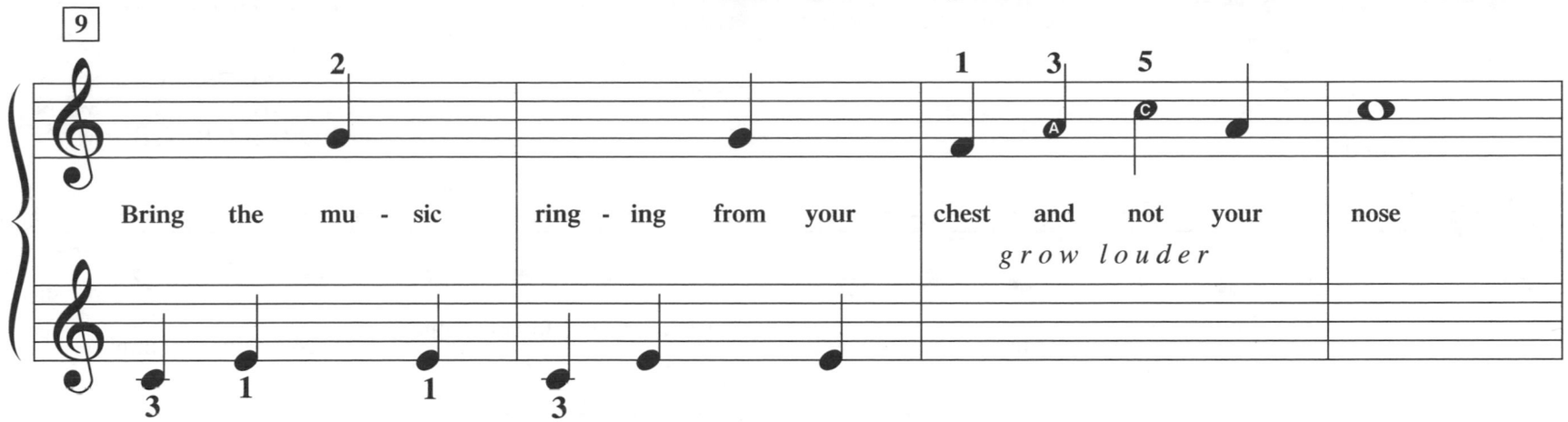

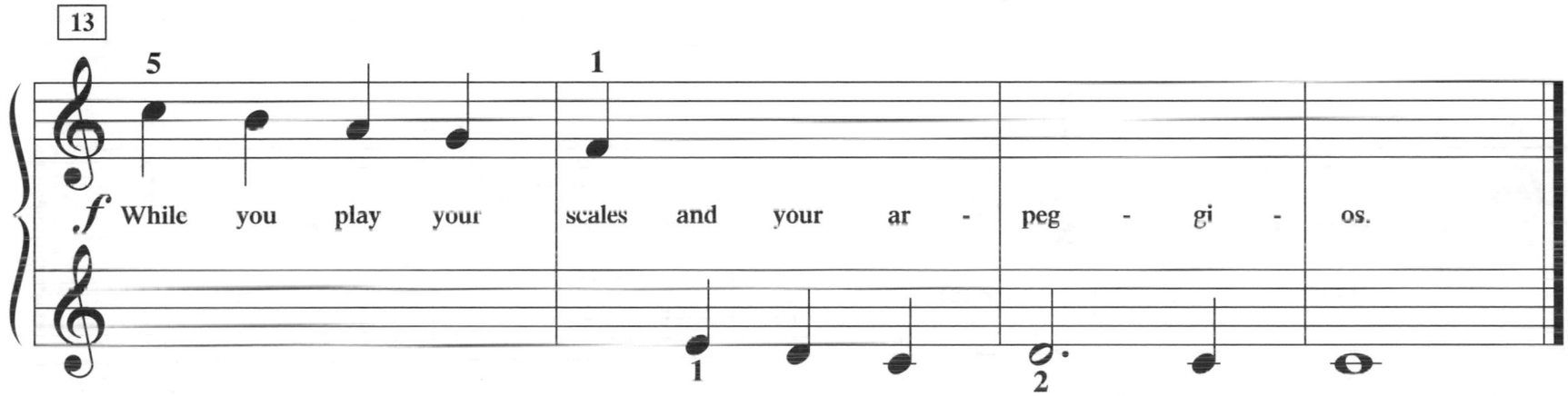

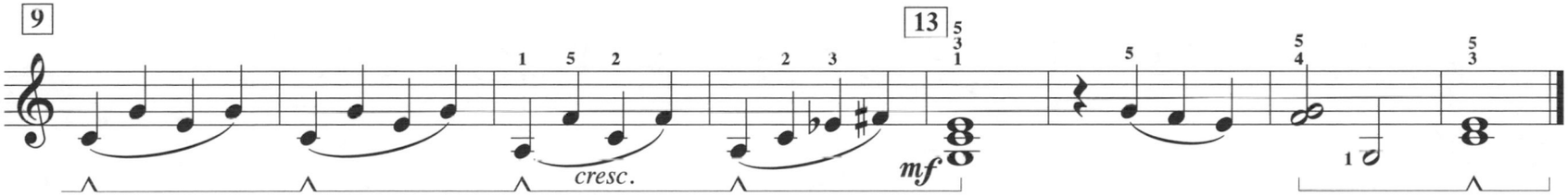

ANSWER: Berlioz

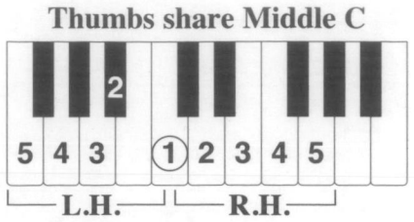

WHO SAID THIS?
You think. You wink. You do a double blink. You close your eyes and jump.

Step in Time

from *Mary Poppins*

Words and Music by
RICHARD M. SHERMAN
and ROBERT B. SHERMAN

With spirit

f Kick your knees up, Link your el - bows, Step in Time! Kick your knees up, Link your el - bows, Step in Time!

5

Never need (a) rea - son, never need (a) rhyme, Kick your knees up, Link your el - bows, Step in Time!

Teacher Duet: (Student plays 1 octave higher)

R.H.

L.H. *mf*

© 1963 Wonderland Music Company, Inc.
Copyright Renewed.
All Rights Reserved. Used by Permission.

ANSWER: Bret